Saving Fiona

The Story of the World's Most Famous Baby Hippo

Thane Maynard,
Director of the Cincinnati Zoo
& Botanical Garden

Houghton Mifflin Harcourt
Boston New York

Additional photographs:
p. 42 bottom © Enate Images/Shutterstock.com
p. 43 bottom © J. Stephen Hicks/keepsake RF/Corbis
p. 43 top © Alan and Sandy Carey/Photodisc/Getty Images
p. 44 left © UryadnikovS/Fotolia
p. 45 top © Natalie Anthes/iStockphoto.com
p. 45 left © Jupiterimages/PHOTOS.com/Getty Images
p. 44 top © Mike Stadnyckyj/iStockphoto.com/Getty Images
p. 44 bottom © Michele Burgess/keepsake RF/Corbis
p. 45 bottom © Digital Vision/Getty Images

hmhco.com

The text type was set in Avenir Book.
The display type was set in Puggo.

Library of Congress Cataloging-in-Publication Data is on file.
ISBN 978-1-328-48513-7

Manufactured in China
SCP 10 9 8 7 6 5 4 3 2 1
4500701339

This book is dedicated to all the members of
#TeamFiona
who worked tirelessly to save baby Fiona.
You showed the world the incredible
commitment, teamwork, and tenacity it takes
to give animals the care they deserve.

This is Fiona.
She is a baby hippopotamus,
but not just any baby hippopotamus.

She is the first premature
hippopotamus to be
raised by humans.

She is a survivor.
This is her story.

There had not been hippos at the Cincinnati Zoo
& Botanical Garden for 20 years.

People really love hippos; their big, round bodies and storybook
appeal made them the most requested animal at the zoo. When
the zoo planned to build a new African animal habitat, making
a space for the hippos was a top priority.

One thing hippos need is water. Lots and lots of water. The water in the 70,000-gallon hippo pool in Hippo Cove is 100 percent rainwater, collected and saved every time it rains in Cincinnati. To keep the water clear so visitors are always able to see the hippos from all sides, the zoo makes use of the biggest pool filter in town!

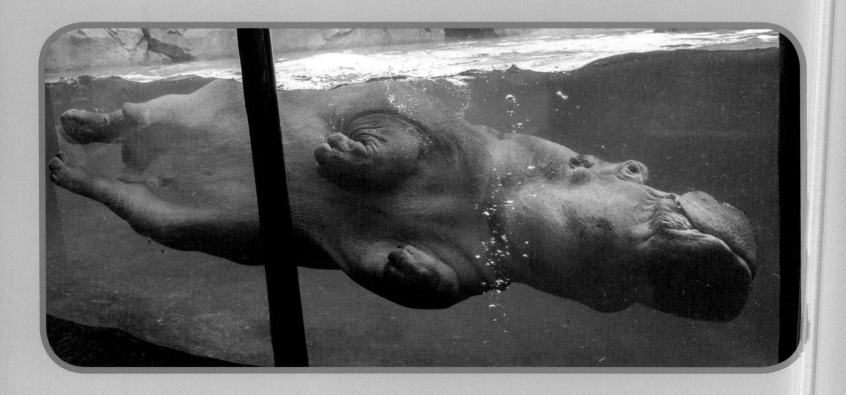

The first residents of Hippo Cove were 17-year-old Bibi and 34-year-old Henry. They arrived in 2016.

Bibi had only lived with female hippopotamuses; Henry was the first male hippo she'd ever seen.

Henry had lived with many hippos, male and female. He had even fathered some babies.

Everyone hoped that Bibi and Henry would get along and have some babies of their own.

Not long after the pair was introduced, there was good news. Bibi and Henry were going to be parents!

Scientists from the zoo's research team conducted the world's first ultrasound on a Nile hippopotamus.

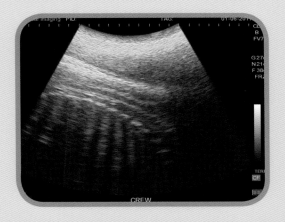

Because hippos have a thick layer of fat to insulate them for their life in the water, nobody was sure if the ultrasound would even work. But a scientist slid under Bibi's huge belly, and sure enough, you could see a spinal cord and even little hippo feet!

The zoo staff continued to monitor Bibi throughout her pregnancy. Soon there would be a baby hippopotamus at the Cincinnati Zoo.

But sometimes things happen *too* soon. Bibi's caregivers noticed that though it was two months early, Bibi was acting as though she was going to give birth. She had no appetite. She was swimming continuously and doing barrel rolls. Her body showed signs of labor.

They rushed to her area in Hippo Cove where they got a big surprise. Even though Bibi wasn't due to give birth until March, lying there on the ground was the littlest hippo anybody had ever seen.

It was January 24, 2017.

At only 29 pounds, the baby hippo was about the size of a heavy football. Hippos are normally three times that size at birth and very active. In the wild, hippos are born in the water and can climb right up onto their mom's back. They even nurse underwater.

This little hippo had the entire team shocked.

Being a preemie, the baby just lay there. She was too weak to stand and certainly couldn't climb. A first-time mother, Bibi looked at the baby with mild curiosity.

There was no time to waste. The zoo's care team jumped into action. They picked up the baby and started to warm her with thick blankets.

Everyone had lots of questions:

What do we feed her?

Should we put her in the water?

How do we make her stronger?

How would a hippo mom take care of a premature baby in the wild?

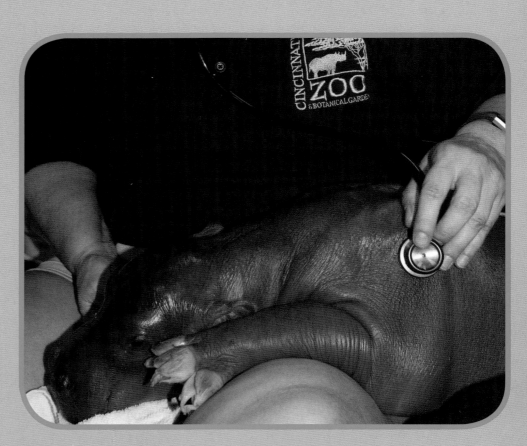

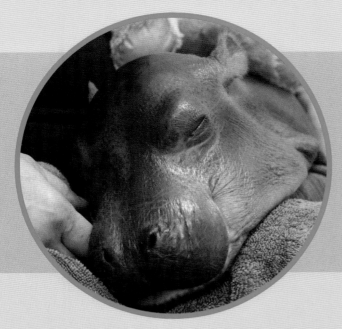

Nobody had ever raised a premature hippo. If Fiona was going to survive, everybody who would be taking care of her would have to learn everything one day at a time.

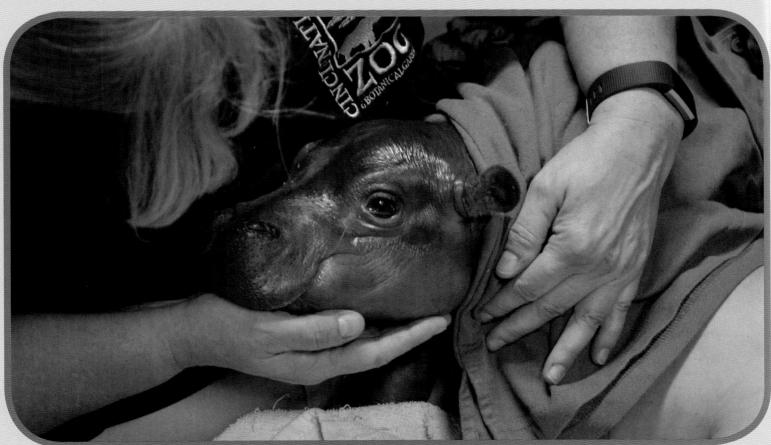

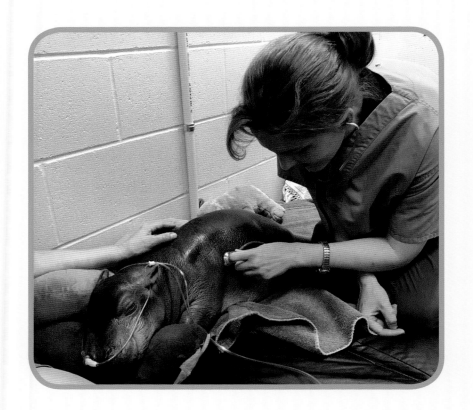

A team of specialized caregivers was assembled, including the zoo's hippo keepers, a nursery staff of baby animal experts, and an Animal Health team of veterinarians, veterinary technicians, and the zoo nutritionist.

#TeamFiona was committed to saving the baby hippo's life, whatever it took.

After talking it over, they decided to name the female baby hippo Fiona, after the lovable princess with the wiggly ears from the movie *Shrek*.

The zoo decided to share Fiona's struggles with the world via social media. Everyone soon fell in love with the little hippo. They rooted for her and sent support and positive vibes her way when she needed them most.

#TeamFiona grew and grew.

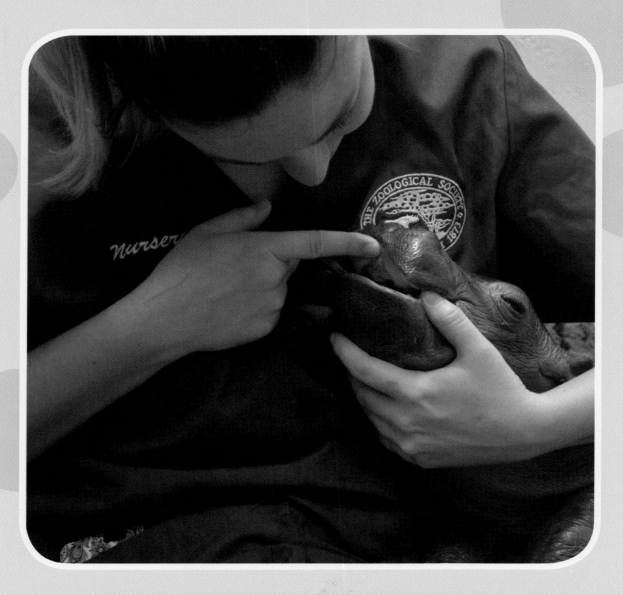

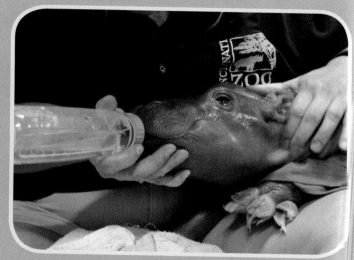

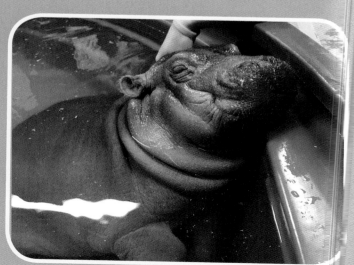

The team knew that someone had to stay with the baby around the clock, literally holding her to keep her warm.

A special area in the hippo barn was set aside for the baby to live in until she began to grow. The building had a heated floor and the heat in the room was cranked up to 98 degrees to make sure she didn't get chilled.

Even her little pool became a hot tub,
filled with water of nearly 100 degrees.

The first dilemma was getting Fiona to nurse. As is the case with all infant mammals, it would be best for Fiona to drink her mother's milk. But Bibi is HUGE—over 3,100 pounds—and tiny Fiona couldn't reach her to nurse.

The team found the biggest breast pump on the market, but that idea didn't work.

So a scientist slid under Bibi again—just like they had when they first saw Fiona in an ultrasound—and hand-milked her like a cow. The team was able to get some milk.

Fiona was able to drink a little of Bibi's milk, giving her important antibodies from her mom. And the zoo's nutritionist sent milk samples off for analysis to the milk repository at the National Zoo in Washington, DC. They learned, for the first time, that hippo milk is much higher in protein and lower in fat than human milk. So every day a special formula was mixed up and heated for Fiona to drink.

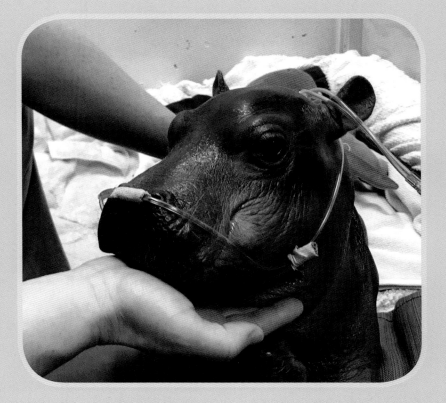

But it was difficult to keep Fiona interested in feeding.

And sometimes she would have a difficult time breathing.

You can imagine how much Fiona did not like the oxygen tube, or cannula, in her nose!

The zoo's nursery keepers know that the keys to raising a healthy baby animal are making sure the baby gains weight and stays hydrated. At about one month old, Fiona wasn't looking so good. She didn't have much energy, she wasn't eating, and, even worse, she wasn't keeping down what little food she did eat.

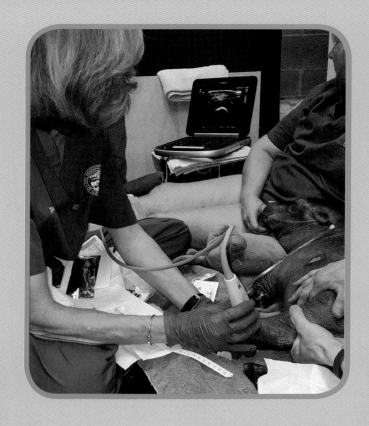

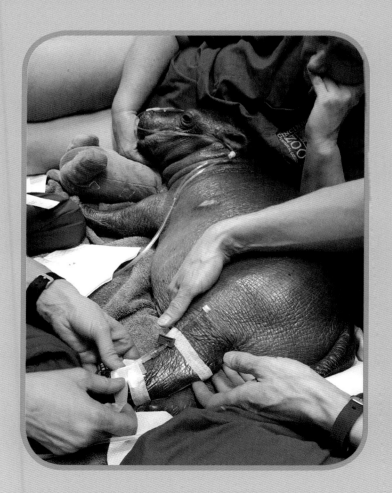

It takes a village to raise a premature hippo. Someone on the zoo staff shared that when her own daughter was sick and needed fluids, her hospital called in a specialized vascular access team to find her tiny veins—and her daughter recovered.

So when the zoo reached out to the Cincinnati Children's Hospital, they sent their special VAT nurses right over—to put in a hippo IV.

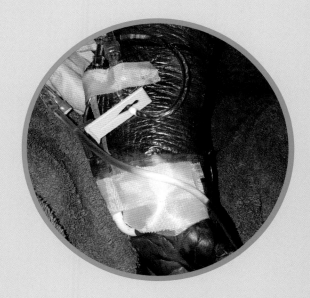

It took a couple of tries because Fiona pulled the first one out, but eventually the IV stayed in for a week and Fiona was finally well hydrated. She started gaining weight and becoming more active.

Fiona had turned a corner.

Fiona began putting on two to three pounds a day and graduated two more pool sizes as she grew. Once she was a few months old, she began living in the area adjacent to her mother and father so the family could begin bonding.

At this stage in her young life, Fiona still spent much of her time with her keepers and other members of **#TeamFiona** who would swim with her, play with her to give her some exercise, and feed her bottles of specially prepared formula. It was the only way to keep her healthy.

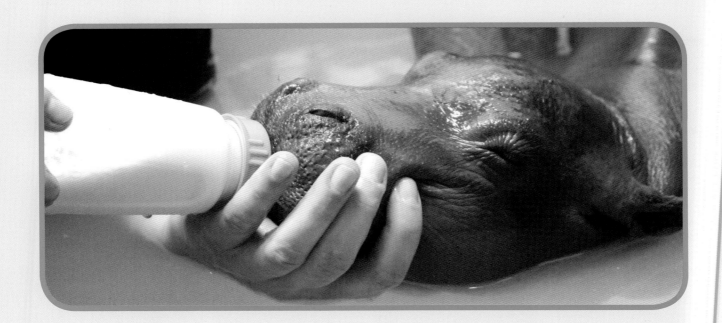

The team was encouraged by Fiona's progress, but at the same time everyone was worried about the risks involved in reuniting her with Bibi and Henry. After all, the parents weighed over 7,000 pounds combined, and Fiona was still *so* little.

Her caregivers and the zoo's mammal curator worked up a step by step plan for Fiona. She began by learning to push off the bottom of the big indoor pool, chaperoned by keepers in case she couldn't navigate the deeper water or get to the surface to breathe.

Then Fiona started spending time with Bibi indoors, giving them a chance to get to know each other better without the risk of water.

Fiona did amazing things with Bibi, such as exploring her mouth (which made everybody a bit nervous!), and Bibi was proving to be a great hippo mom.

The world celebrated these milestones right along with Fiona's care team. People couldn't get enough of the videos and photos that the zoo shared via social media. They demanded a daily **#FionaFix**.

The next big hurdle was the outdoor pool, where the water is nine feet deep. Little Fiona was less than two feet tall, and even though hippos spend all day in the water, resting and staying cool, they can't actually swim. They are so dense they would sink right to the bottom.

Instead, they walk along the bottom of rivers and pools and propel their bodies to the water's surface to breathe. An adult hippo can hold its breath for about five minutes, but Fiona's lungs were not developed enough to do that.

So at first, Fiona would go out with her keepers, which was as much fun for them as for her! Hippos are built for a life in the water and the keepers soon saw that Fiona was no exception—

she loved the pool!

Then came the big day everyone had looked forward to, with a little sadness. When Fiona was about four months old it was time to let her explore the big pool with Bibi.

This would mean the end to the daily swimming and contact with her keepers, who had raised her since her unexpected beginning.

Fiona did great with her mom and had fun in the pool, playing and
bouncing around underwater every day. It was clear that her keepers
missed her more than she missed them, which is a good thing since
she will spend her life with hippos, not people!

The grand finale was the family reunion, when Henry, Bibi, and Fiona started spending time in the pool together. Fiona continued to play and be a very active "little" hippo—by the time she was six months old, she weighed over four hundred pounds.

Sometimes Fiona settles down in the shallow end of her pool, staying cool while she takes a nap.

Everyone at the Cincinnati Zoo agrees that we've learned a lot from Fiona. We feel like we are experts on hippo ultrasounds, hippo milk, and everything else you need to know to raise a premature baby hippo for the first time.

But mostly we learned that love carries the day and makes the impossible possible. Fiona taught us all to never give up.

Hooray for Hippos!

There are two species of hippopotamus: the Nile hippo and the pygmy hippo. They both live in Africa.

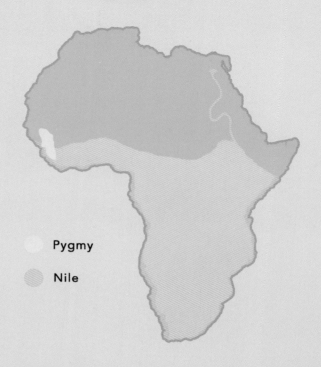

Pygmy

Nile

Pygmy hippos (below) are much smaller, weighing 500–600 pounds. Pygmy hippos are very rare and come from limited forested river areas in the West African countries of Liberia, Sierra Leone, and Ivory Coast.

Fiona and her family are **Nile hippos**— the big kind (above). They can grow super huge. Female hippos are typically between 3,000 and 4,000 pounds, and males can weigh up to 4,000–5,000 pounds. Sometimes male hippos reach 7,000 pounds, but that's an exceptionally big animal.

- A group of hippos is called a *bloat*.

- The word *hippopotamus* comes from the Greek word that means "river horse," even though its closest relative is a whale, not a horse!

- Hippos once lived in most of Africa, except the Sahara Desert. Today Nile hippos don't have as much room because there are so many more people, but they still live in a wide range of protected areas, national parks, and other wetland and river areas in East and Southern Africa.

- Hippos are built for a life in the water. They appear so big because they actually have a thick layer of fat under their skin that insulates them like a wetsuit, since they spend all day submerged in water. Also, like many aquatic animals, hippos have their eyes, nose, and ears all on top of their heads so they can breathe and use their senses while submerged.

Hippos have special mucous glands that secrete a red oily fluid that protects their skin from sunburn and drying, and perhaps from infection. The fluid is called *blood sweat* but it isn't really blood or sweat. In fact, unlike humans and horses, hippos don't have sweat glands.

Hippos can open their mouths 150 degrees wide, about three times wider than humans can.

Male hippos are very competitive, so they like to mark their territories to warn other males where they have been. To accomplish this, they spray their poop in a behavior called dung-showering in which they spin their tail like a propeller as they poop. Sometimes this involves two males approaching each other in the water, staring at each other threateningly, and then turning their tails toward each other and letting their poop fly!

A male hippo's tusks grow up to 1½ feet long!

Hippos can run faster than humans, reaching speeds of up to 18 miles per hour on land.

Hippos are herbivores, which means they only eat plants. They don't eat in the water but come out at night to forage for grasses and bushes for their dinner. Sometimes they will walk three or four miles in a single night looking for enough to eat.

Hippos appear friendly, but they can be dangerous! Since they are herbivores, they do not attack people to eat them. However, when they come out at night they often encounter people; since they can weigh 5,000 pounds, it can be catastrophic if they just run into a person! Most of the conflicts between people and hippos happen when hippos wander into farm fields or gardens near their river homes and people run out to scare them away.

A Note from Thane Maynard

In my 40 years in the zoo field I have never seen such massive interest and an outpouring of love and encouragement for one animal like I have seen for Fiona. Some of it is her "saved from the brink" story. And some is due to social media. But everybody who knows her will tell you that there really is something special about Fiona. She is one of a kind and a symbol of hope to people of all ages all over the world.

Fiona celebrates her first birthday.